Culver City Centennial Poetry Collection

Culver **CITY**
CENTENNIAL
CELEBRATION

September 20, 1917 – September 20, 2017

Edited by
Dr. Janet Cameron Hoult
Honorary Artist Laureate for Poetry

outskirts
press

DEDICATION

To Culver City
May the next 100 years
be filled with wonderful things
to celebrate
at your
Bicentennial in 2117...!

Janet Cameron Moult

FOREWORD

Culver City completed its one-year Centennial Celebration on September 20, 2017 exactly 100 years from the day Harry Culver received his City Charter. The year included many community events such as a parade, birthday party-in-the-park, and formal incorporation ceremony with the Culver family.

During the year celebration we all searched for words which could describe the pride and enjoyment we have experienced living in Culver City. Words alone did not always describe the strong emotional attachment many of us have had with the City. Dr. Janet Hoult filled that gap. She organized a poetry contest inviting residents to create poems commemorating our Centennial. The result was poetry which evoked, as simple words could not, the emotional response that we felt, but had difficulty articulating.

Thank you, Janet, for providing our now and future community with the essence of Culver City.

Paul A. Jacobs
President, Culver City Centennial Celebration Committee
Former Mayor and City Councilmember

Table of Contents

My Centennial Summer
BY STEVEN GELB

Just like the Olympics Quadrennial,
I celebrate Culver's Centennial!
There was lots to do,
I will mention a few,
Like concerts and walks,
They're perennial.

I went to some concerts, just four,
At City Hall, they're no bore!
I heard Country and jazz,
And some hot razzmatazz,
I sure could hear all the crowd roar!

I went on a walk through Vets' Park.
But just when I thought it a lark,
From behind that there tree,
Jumped a dog big as me,
And, brother, how loud he could bark!

On Saturdays I danced at the Center,
I felt there much more than a renter.
With those Big Bands in tow,
I went with the flow.
And danced till my muscles were tender!

Thus ends my Centennial Summer.
It all was quite a big stunner.
From now looking back,
I found a great knack,
To look more and more as a comer.

Culver City History

A City Named Culver—A Tribute from an Outsider
BY B.T. KHANH

Machado and Sepulveda, Ince and Higuera,
names that come alive as I unveil the 'story
of a place called Culver City .
Two low-land "ranchos"; a creek, La Ballona;
a modest start, no doubt, but look where It is now .
a five square mile spread, with a border so unruly
it may run through properties and give them split personality .
A prized piece in the urban puzzle of the surrounding Metropolis ,
a city within a city ?! Most definitely,
dotted with parks,
museums and historical landmarks,
an Art District...not to mention
a theater housed in an old train substation ,
a Main street, too… though admittedly
the shortest in the country !
And to top it all ,
Wedge-shaped and standing tall,
a Hotel named Culver,
a six-story "skyscraper",
favorite hangout of movie stars famous the world over.
"Heart of Screenland"''
summarizes its stand
scrolled across the City Seal,
showcasing its flashy appeal,
and bearing testimony
to a thriving entertainment industry.
A Star, a City was born in nineteen seventeen,
because a man named Harry Culver had a dream
and brought it to reality !
Little did I know about Culver City
when I moved into the vicinity.
Now the City is about to celebrate its Centennial,
I am celebrating too,
because you see, I live in the "Culver City… adjacent"
and as the advertisement goes: "All roads lead to Culver City."

Ghosts in the Culver Hotel's Basement

BY RON COHEN

They all left their crypts, graves and tombs at the stroke of midnight of
September 20th, 2017 to celebrate Culver City's Centennial.
"All roads lead to Culver City", proclaimed once Harry Culver
But tonight all roads lead to the basement of the Culver Hotel.

They all made it on time at midnight, without exception.
Along mahogany tables they sat. Tears of joy in their eyes.
Harry Culver at the head of the table, shaking hands, all smiles
And by his side a young Howard Hughes exchanging greetings
   with the owners of Rancho La Ballona, Rancho Rincon
   and with Chief "Red Blood", the representative of the Tongva Native Americans
   of the original Culver City.
John Wayne, "Duke", a former owner of the Culver Hotel
   sat alongside Paul Helm of the famous Helms Bakery.
Even the old Mariner holding the Helm left Chase Park to attend.

They all waited anxiously for the grand entrance of the king to preside
 And he finally did arrive —
 Leo the Lion — dressed in a black tuxedo.
He gave three loud roars and the meeting came to order.

They all came together to celebrate Culver City's Centennial:
 Judy Garland of "The Wizard of Oz",
 Clark Gable discussing the making of "Gone With The Wind",
 Johnny Weissmuller demonstrating his famous Tarzan Yell.
 Lassie and its owner sat side by side
 and E.T. walked among the guests and extended his famous two fingers.
 Batman, Bruce Lee and the Green Hornet all came dressed in costume.
 Charlton Heston rode in on his Ben Hur chariot
 and Liz Taylor wore her Cleopatra outfit.
They all filled the basement until it was standing room only.

Harry Culver got up and raised a golden champagne glass and made a toast.
All the invited guests who were part of Culver City's history followed suit:
"Today we celebrate the Centennial of Culver City", "The Heart of Screenland"

Though we are not here physically, we definitely are here in spirit.
We all contributed to the growth of this jewel of a city.
I thank you all sincerely and bid you may all rest in peace for you will all be
invited again for Culver City's Bi-Centennial."

The next morning, the doors to the Culver Hotel were wide open...the hotel staff
rushed from place to place and from room to room to make sure everything was
ready for the day's scheduled events..
A deafening silence welcomed them as they descended to the basement.

On the basement floor was a rolled parchment tied with a green ribbon,
an invitation to hundreds of V.I.P.s from Culver City's glorious past.
The staff shrugged their shoulders and did not know what to make of it.
They placed the rolled parchment in the attic together with old furniture
And other relics and memorabilia from the hotel's magnificent past.

And then they heard an eerie echo resonating through the entire hotel.
"Happy Centennial Culver City and all the best. May you grow and thrive.
We are looking forward to the next hundred years, holding our breath.
We will be there to celebrate the Bi-Centennial, if not physically, then in spirit.
But we will definitely be there!"

They Aren't Here Anymore

BY HELEN SEID

At the **Rollerdrome** we'd go round and round
A wonderful place to skate
And who would think a little park
Would someday become its fate.

And everyone went to **Stern's** for their famous Bar-B-Q
Whenever I went there I always saw everyone I knew
That secret recipe is all but lost, known only by a few
And so we settle for other places, we'll have to make them do.

Many people would go to **Red Riding Stables**
To board or ride a horse
And down the road was the **go cart track**
Where you would drive their winding course.

The Dairy on Sepulveda is where I'd stop for milk
and other quick supplies
I could drive right thru but then one day
It vanished right before my eyes.

At the start of each summer
To **Kirkpatrick's** I'd go to buy a new bathing suit
From room to room and down the aisles
To find one that was just so cute.

To the **Studio Drive In** we took the kids
With them in their P.J.'s
And during the movie they'd fall asleep
Hurrah for the good old days.

Before a picnic I'd make a quest
To **Culver City Ice Co.** to fill my chest
And get some cubes for sodas and such
I really miss it very much.

At the **Ice Arena,** we'd have such fun
Our skates we laced up tight
And try to go both forward and back
To everyone's delight.

The **Roll & Rye** was the neighborhood deli
For pastrami or corned beef on rye
And chicken soup and chopped liver
It was so hard to say good-bye.

Ship's Coffee Shop its sign so high
With toasters on the table
For breakfast it could not be beat
You could toast yourself a bagel.

In Culver Center, there was **JCPenny's** and
Grant's Five and Ten
In the days when a dime could buy you something
We'll never see that again.

And in Studio Village we had **Newberry's**
Another five and dime
And they even had a lunch counter
Where we could sit and "dine".

Put your sign in the window, and listen for his whistle
The **Helmsman** will be coming by
I'd run to his truck to buy cookies and cakes
Jelly donuts and Banana Cream Pie. Yum, Yum!

If I missed your favorite I'm sorry
But aren't you glad you came
Along with me for this little trip
Down Culver City's memory lane.

They're all gone now, I miss them so
There's nothing left to see
The only place they still exist is in my memory.

Helms Bakery
BY ANGIE WALLER

Early morning
Cool and crisp
The air is bulging
With the yeasty aroma
Of baking bread.

The loaves are loaded
Into waiting vans
The wheaty smell
Wafting from them
As they spread out
Along the dawn-dappled
Streets of Culver City
And L.A.
Delivering breakfast—
Breads and bagels
Danish and donuts
Brought to one's door
Fresh from Helms Bakery.

Once—but no more:
Now there are stores
And cafes with patios
New aromas to tantalize
Still the sign remains
Atop the historic
Zigzag Moderne façade
A reminder of the
Delicious days of
"Olympic Bread".

The Culver City Rollerdrome

BY MO DE KOFF

Quickly down Washington Place I scurried
a small red metal skate case by my side
    while safely tucked near new
      still nestled heel to toe
were my Mom's white leather skates size five

How my excitement grew as I hurried
for soon there'd be smooth wooden floors to glide
    don't ask me how I knew
      just twelve but I can go
to the Rollerdrome—a Quonset-hut hive

Buzzing like bees on a giant round rim
the skaters take strides to the organ's song
    girls only—now gents too
      then couples take the floor
backward/forward—skaters whirling like tops

A glitter ball is spinning as lights dim
there's true magic here but it won't last long
    a child in Xanadu
      comes of age in folklore
memories blur as skaters twirl while time stops

The Progression of Culver City

BY LAUREN SEBEROS

It all began with one man's journey to the Golden State.
Harry Culver wanted to learn more about the real estate.
Palms became a part of L.A.
Culver said nay.
Now it was 1916 when the first elementary school was created.
After a while the name and school faded.
It was rebuilt and many of you know it as Linwood E. Howe.
We finally reach 1917, the birth of Culver City now.

A couple of years later the Roaring Twenties took over.
There were new events happening bringing it to a transitioning Culver.
The Culver Hotel was in its beginning stages.
Several agreements and laws were signed on various pages
Which would lead to great buildings and familiar faces
Like the famous Helm's bakery and the Wizard of Oz.
1949 marked the beginning of the school district
                    and Adolph Steller's industrial cause.
More and more of Culver's schools opened their doors.
Doris Hechinger composed the city's first score.
The Olympic marathon runners dashed through the city in 1984.
Eventually the entertainment industry got updated with a new name and more.
Sony Pictures, what a gem it truly has become,
Home to some of the greatest movies that have ever been done.

Now we are today standing in a city
        of greatness, wonder
          and amazing feats.
No other city is like Culver and it can't be beat!

My Kind of Town

BY RUTH BERMAN

I'm not a citizen of Culver City
May as well be… what a pity!
All my activities gravitate there
And some of them I will gladly share…

The Culver Hotel
Graduations, weddings, galas galore
Goes on and on and much, much more

And the studios, Culver and Sony
Where classical movies are made
Have been around forever and never will fade

The city parks, so special for children to play
They all look so happy I must say

The Culver City Plunge, so inviting and warm
Where folks from all over will swarm

Ah yes, the Senior Center offering all kinds of classes,
Keeps brains active for all of the masses

I love watching the Metro shooting through town
Whoever thought of this deserves a king's crown

The Police and Fire Departments so efficiently run
If an accident happens how quickly they come

Culver City is a happy place to live
Seems like people give and give

I truly think I have said enough
Gosh, not living in Culver City sure is tough

CULVER CITY—*Historical Acrostic*

BY RON COHEN

C ulver City, "The Heart of Screenland", once the home of The Culver Studios, Columbia Pictures, MGM and now Sony Pictures.

U ltimately, "All roads lead to Culver City", is the way Harry Culver advertised the city in 1917, when he founded the city which covers five square miles and has 40,000 residents.

L ong ago the Tongva Native Americans, a hunter-gatherer society, lived in this area for 8000 years in peace and dignity next to their neighbors the Chumash Indians to the North and West of them.

V enues of interest include: The Culver Hotel, Helms Bakery, West L.A College, Holy Cross and Hillside cemeteries of the stars, Fox Hills Mall and the Kirk Douglas Theatre.

E xpo-line takes you to Union Station, China Town, Olvera Street, Hollywood Highland, The Queen Mary, LAX and Downtown Santa Monica and don't forget the reliable Culver City Bus.

R elax and dine in Culver City's fine restaurants, stroll along its downtown streets, take in a movie at the ArcLight theatre and watch a world premiere play at the Kirk Douglas theatre.

C ount your blessings and be glad that you live in this pearl of a city, a jewel in the crown of West L.A.

I n time you will retire and the Culver City Senior Center will be waiting for you to enrich your life with social activities, a hot lunch, and a place to learn, play, dance, exercise, watch movies, be entertained and socialize.

T ake your time and visit the city's many attractions, schools, libraries, shopping centers and activity centers. Swim in its public swimming pool and enjoy its many beautiful parks.

Y ou won't regret the fact that you chose Culver City as your primary residence, because here you will thrive, prosper, grow and enjoy a good quality of life.

Culver City Seal

BY LESLIE L. LENELL

Movies, Lantana, Bear and Sun
Imprinted on the Culver City Seal.
Here is the Heart of Screenland;
A little city that's lots of fun.

Happy Birthday to our City Seal.
It has been used for eighty years.
A super symbol of united people,
WE salute you with great zeal!

Arf Arcy the Seal Returns to Culver City

BY MARSHA WILDE

Hey — you —
You! I said, you — hey!
Whatcha doin' flappin' 'round in that pool?
That ain't no bathing pool!
It's a public beauty pool … ya know,
to add to the public beauty of Culver City —
of the Vets' Memorial, in fact ….
What's your name?
        Arf!
Arf? What kind of name is that?
Oh, I get it now, A-R-F … You are that seal.
My friend who works with me told me about you.
I couldn't see you properly before.
My eyes ain't too good and I gotta get new glasses.
Just found out my insurance won't pay for 'em, either!
Anyway, hey seal, you gotta get outta there.
Absolutely No Bathing Allowed.
        ARF!
Well Arf, ya gotta climb outta there right now.
Somebody see you in there, we **both** be in trouble!
Here, I'll help you out.
Man, them flippers is something else, ain't they?
        Arf — aaarrrfff!
Man, beautiful. Strong.
Why, I bet you cut through the water something fierce!
        Arrff!
Well — fierce AND beautiful, I mean.
WOW! Big Boy, you're one cool shiny dude.
You really are!
Trouble is, Arf, ya can't keep flappin' 'round in that there pool.
        ARF! ARF! ARF!
Are ya trying to say Culver's Number One? Betcha are.
And you're right, handsome seal. The city's got you AND a city seal.
        Aarrf! Aarrff!

Culver City

BY DAVID KATZ

At this time of my life
As I walk the sidewalks that have been somewhat
  uprooted by the trees on Jefferson
I think back about my life in Culver City
The bridge of my life is long and sweet and short
One moment I'm opening up new boxes in the house
The next minute my step-son is grown

I walk and I think about the pathways of my life of the city that I've grown to
love
Markets and city stores, parks, restaurants
These are the places that I have warm feelings about
Things are changing and moving
The rain and the sunshine in the clouds come and go
But as I walk further I reflect on the wind that blows the leaves from the trees

My heart opens
My eyes are wide open
There is a whirlwind of emotions
As I think and feel
The wonder of living here for 36 years
Merging into my soul
Like a great mist
Is the life I have lived in Culver City

The sweetness, the sadness, the sentimental
I can hear the rustling of the leaves, the trees, the wind
As I walk
The feelings get hot
They boil up
Inside of me
Walking and reflecting
Again I see in my mind
All the warm
Celebrations with my wife and friends over the years

Bright
Flowers
Sunshine
I close my eyes
Images of my life
Flying over Culver City
And then it rains

I walk on
The clouds open up
I feel I am one raindrop
In this Huge universe and here in Culver City
I want that raindrop to remain
One raindrop, just one

I look at my hands
I see friendship and smiles that have greeted me throughout my life in Culver
City
Soft sunshine warms my face
Dancing, writing, drawing
Feeling all these things
The smiles and the laughter that move from each street to street
I know this city
I love this city
It sings with me every day
I keep walking and I can feel and remember
The bike rides, the jogging, walking up the hill with my wife
The fourth of July fireworks
Colors and fantasies and dreams that I have lived

I walk on
I remember
There is passion and love in every street in this city
Where I have slept,
I have wept,
I have dreamed,
I have lived and
I have loved.

Culver City
Organizations / Institutions / Services

So Many Sisters!
BY PAT HARMON

I have always wanted a sister;
Alas, I was an only child.
I thought I had no sisters
But in Culver City I discovered
I have sisters, four of them.
They have whole cities they
Bring with them in sisterhood.

My sisters live in Canada and Japan.
They live in South Korea and Mexico.
And, if I didn't have enough sisters already,
I might get a friendly sister from Italy. **

They say they will share their world
With me in Culver City and I promise
I will share my Culver City with them.
There is a committee that knows all
About my sisters. Maybe I will join
If you need more sisters
      so should you.

** Capo d'Orlando, Italy became Sister City number 5 in 2017

Missing Italy

BY LYRA BRODY SMALL

Because of the gelato — Because of the Mediterranean Sea
Because of Pass It On — Because of the paper store
Because of the jokes Jim tells — Because of the pizza
Because of the pasta — Because there are no rules when it comes to driving
Because of the granita — Because of the Leaning Tower of Pisa
Because of the museums — Because of the chalk paintings
Because of the sculptures — Because of the ballet
Because of the islands just off the coast of it — Because of Little Sicily
Because of the parks — Because of the nice kids — Because of the apartments
Because it's Italy.

VARIETY at The Julian Dixon Library

BY TERRY DICKS

The old folks said,
"It takes all kinds to build a world."
I see that now…sitting here in the *Julian Dixon Library* of Culver City
I see…
Students with markers, heads bent—
The studious and those playing computer games.
The elderly relaxing in chairs with magazines and books,
Toddlers sitting on the rug engrossed in imagination
A homeless man carrying a plastic bag of stuff.
And some who are just getting out of the storm outside.

All are quietly sitting surrounded by thousands of books.
Books stacked neatly and catalogued
Some new, many old
Filled with the wisdom of the ages.

I am at peace in this depository of knowledge
I love sitting in the quiet
Previewing my own stack of books
And should I mention my favorite chair?
It's blue with eight inches of soft padding.
Oh how I love this chair…I *always* sit here.
Now and then, I look around.
I see the variety of folks
There is beauty here
There's love here too
From the kind librarians to the people sitting nearby
Kindness exudes.
I know because I feel it every time I come.

The variety of people are like decoration
Making this quiet place come alive.
This is where life flows.

The old folks wisely knew,
It takes all kinds to build a world.

Summer at the Culver City Library

BY PAT HARMON

The Culver City Library is buzzing.
The Summer Reading Program is here
Children are coming by the dozen.
All prizes to win, except no beer.
They read and read and count the books.
And write them down when finished.
Prizes awarded daily, not on looks.
Reading pleasures are not diminished.
There are plays too every week.
We tell stories from far and wide.
Get here early for a good seat
So you don't end up back outside.
Julian Dixon would be very proud
To see his library so endowed.

Culver City Schools and the SSYHC

BY JOANNE WOLF

Culver City is a special place.
We call it a "Shining Star".
It offers much to all of us,
It's on the highest level of the bar.

One of it's greatest assets
Is the Culver City Schools.
They are known to be very fine
Above average — That's the rules.

Elementary schools, we have five
To help our children grow,
To learn and blossom to their best
And increase how much they know.

The schools have Sports and Music programs
And special groups and interest clubs,
And personal and group talents
Are advanced at special hubs.

The Sandy Segal Youth Health Center
Is where problems get talked about
In a place that's safe and confidential
And the teens are sure there is no doubt

That the therapists are there JUST for them.
No problems are too great
To talk about, then resolve
What's on the Student's plate.

The Interns work and really care
And help students in every session
To increase confidence in themselves
And help make a good progression.

The Center helps so many students
To grow and find their way.
We're lucky OUR High School has this place—
It's a haven that brightens each day.

It is a Gold Star on our list
Of Special Services Culver City's proud to give.
We're so glad Culver City's our home—
It's where WE choose to live.

Culver City Y.M.C.A.

BY PAT HARMON

Thank you, it's what I say
Keeping me active every day
Helping diseases stay away.
Connecting my core as I lay
Doing yoga, it's my way.
So, Culver City Y.M.C.A.
I will continue to pay, pay, pay.

Culver City's Caring Corps
BY NORMA GLICKMAN

When you've reached
the time of life
when the hospital Emergency Room
becomes a familiar, revolving door —
and the Paramedics know you by name —
it is fitting, indeed, to sing praises
of their performance.

During the many times when my brother and I
have had to call 911 —
when fighting for breath — or
losing consciousness — and when —
having barely hung up the telephone —
already hearing the fast approaching sounds
of their ambulance sirens — assuring
me that their unfailing assistance
is once again approaching my front door

But —
once a year — for the past ten years —
the Seniors vs Safety Pool Tournament
takes place at our Senior Center — where
our still robust players have — so far —
been able to beat the pants off
the much younger Paramedics — in a
friendly match.

A Little Kindness
BY MO DE KOFF

It was just a little kindness
A slight nod of recognition
Twinkling eyes and a small shy smile
To lift my spirits for awhile

The kindness of asking to help
And share words of encouragement
To reach out for a human touch
It really didn't take that much

How kind of you to invite me
My, you are especially kind
Your kindness I appreciate
I'll be glad to reciprocate

To you, just a little kindness
That slight nod of recognition
Kind words spoken with that sweet smile
My troubles vanished for awhile

And it put a spring in my step
The dark clouds parted for the sun
It's highly contagious, I've found
Your kindness turned my world around

*Culver City was declared "A City of Kindness" in 2017.

Culver City Police Department
BY JOANNE WOLF

Our Culver City Police Department
Is one of which we're proud.
We can always count on them
Whether alone or in a crowd.

They have a reputation
Of being worthy of our trust
To keep our City free of crime
While being fair and just.

They support our City Fathers.
They watch over our events.
They come whenever they are called.
They give us a "Safety Sense"

Our police are very active
In Outreach Programs for the community,
And they work hard to keep them going
So there's constant continuity.

They have an Explorer Program.
They find the "Safest Routes to School".
They have a Citizen's Police Academy
And a Special Olympics Torch-Relay that's cool.

They have Station Tours and Ride-Alongs
And "Coffee with a Cop".
They're known for their Neighborhood Watch.
The Programs never stop.

They have School Resource Officers
And they have Bicycle Patrols too.
They're there at Holiday events
Watching over us with their crew.

We have Traffic and Parking Programs
That are efficient and effective
And preventing or reducing crime
In our City is reflective

Of the quality of our Police Force.
It's high and steady, that's a fact
So our City's safety and high morale
Is always kept intact.

They are our friends when we're in need
On them we do depend.
We are so proud that they are ours.
Their honor we commend.

Our Culver City Police Officers
All fill our hearts with pride.
We are appreciative of all they do
They're the best — Near, Far and Wide.

Thank you, Culver City Police Department.

Earthquake Preparedness—
Sing Along to the tune of Frere Jacques
BY B.T. KHANH

Californians,
Californians,
Be ready,
for t' next Big One,
Better be prepared now,
Better be prepared now,
Don't you wait,
'til too late!
Are furniture,
Heavy pictures,
well secured
to the wall ?
Don't let them tumble down,
Don't let them tumble down,
and hurt you,
trip you ...down

Water and Food,
Med'cines and Cash,
Do you have ?
For three days ?
And blanket n' eyeglasses,
And blanket n' eyeglasses,
Heavy shoes,
Whistle too.
When the ground shakes,
When the ground shakes,
From windows
Away you stay,
Under a heavy table,
Under a heavy table,
Drop and hold,
Cover and duck!

When the shake stops,
When the shake stops,
Check yourself,
Look around,
Stay tuned to *the* radio,
Stay tuned to *the* radio,
F' **ins**tructions,
n' in**for**mation .
n' **ab**ov' all,
KEEP YOUR COOL !

Small Town, Big Heart

BY SANDRA COOPERSMITH

Having written feature stories for Culver City papers since 2005
I've come across topics that fuel the spirit of this city to thrive,
And you'll frequently find golden threads of kindness twining through
The tapestry of stories it's been my very great pleasure to weave for you.
While there are several examples, space allows me to present just two
And I hope after reviewing them you will agree with me
That our town is a truly kind and caring place to be.

I'll start with The Whole 9 Gallery, which opened on Washington in 2007
And is now on Main Street, where it's been a popular presence since 2011.
For shoppers seeking jewelry and art it exemplifies
Creativity with a conscience as a result of its close ties
To The Peace Project, the humanitarian needs
Of which are served through portions of the sales proceeds
That, among other worthwhile deeds, helped provide crutches
To amputees in Sierra Leone, whose people were in the clutches
Of a devastatingly destructive ten-year civil war.
One-fifth of the world's amputees is a horrific score.

Next, if magic is the art of transformation, L.A. GOAL on Overland Avenue
Is the extraordinary emporium where life-changing events regularly ensue.
Founded almost 50 years ago, this private non-profit agency
Enables its members, age 18 and over, to be the best that they can be,
Thus opening a doorway to hope for those with a developmental disability,
Proof that with patience, love and support, dreams can become reality.
I applaud the dedicated staff and volunteers at this amazing facility,
For their efforts have borne fruit, giving us all an opportunity to learn
That gaining confidence and self-esteem results in great societal return
When fragmented souls are integrated and taught to live a life that's whole —
Kudos, indeed, to the caring hearts that power L.A. GOAL!

It thrills me to write stories that educate and show
The kindness that resides here, something many might not know
With all the global and national negative news resulting in overflow
So in writing this poem for Culver City's Centennial I decided to celebrate

What I consider to be our most important and perhaps least promoted trait
That I've now officially put in writing and am so happy to say out loud:
Namely, it's the kindness that permeates our city that has made me truly proud
To live here since the '80s. Happy birthday! I'm so glad to be a part
Of this beautiful community, the small town with the really big heart.

L.A. GOAL poetry class assignment: Since this is Culver City's Centennial year, write your thoughts expressing why Culver City is special to you.

The primary focus turned out to be the connection with L.A. GOAL, which is located in Culver City. Since each member of the class is an individual with unique perspectives, experiences and insights, a variety of approaches and styles emerged. One poem is, with the exception of two very special words at the end, in a private, magical language that prompts your imagination to soar. Enjoy! Sandra Coopersmith

HAPPY BIRTHDAY, CULVER CITY!
From the poets of L.A. GOAL
Culver City is special because ...

L.A. GOAL is full of inspiration.
We are blessed that we have our teenagers
Come here
Because they teach us their skills
And share how they feel.

They open up their hearts
To show their appreciation
Of our progress
And how much they have learned
From us.

When the teenagers teach us
They give us inspiration
By respecting
Not only the members
But, most importantly,
Teaching us our boundaries
And possibilities.

In Culver City we have many options.
The Culver City Library gives the opportunity
To learn to read

And to understand.
Some of the other members take a risk
To try to do better things with their minds
Because we are strong
And we fight for our freedom.

Our minds take us on a journey
Back in time
No matter what we do
And whether or not we make it rhyme.
That's how we connect
The outside
And inside.
>*Brad*

I like coming to L.A. GOAL.
I graduate Culver City school.
I like going to education.
I like writing sentences.
I here to learn.
Margie used to teach me multiplication
And I went to the library with teenagers.
Maria is a teenager in reading class.
Kris helps with the doors.
He is a friend.
I sing Britney Spears
With teenagers.
I sit with friends at lunch.
I help Petite and Cathy fold calendars, stuff envelopes.
Tuesday I am with Lisa, therapist.
I like coming to L.A. GOAL
>*Jenny*

I like to go to movies
In Culver City
Like Ice Age.
I like coming
To L.A. GOAL

And to do a good job
At the art studio.
> *Patricia*

AMGtbay GWEKISH we RITSAst
GOAKEEMH SOtKbAFBH
QMaDEUWYH
doMaKJHY we so AoyGH
WKIKEO2dH DAY We
OdCe we SotMKH
Poecm loceaiee
CoeMKBRH
Love you
> *Elisa*

IDEAS:
- delicious food, great variety of flavors
- a cultural city in tune with its roots
- strong sense of community, artistic and social
- a city full of helping hands, full of empathy
- fountains and sculptures of youth and love and opportunity

POEM:
A city of flavor rests humbly upon distasteful soil.
This new, arrogant soil wishes to nurture tall plants.
Culver City is a cultured city that is happy with its plants.
"No new plants," says Culver City as it embraces its visitors.
Helping hands frolic freely under the warm coastal sun.
Empathy and love circulate like a lively disease
Injecting creative venom, poisoning city dwellers with joy.
Food is understood in the city, just like its people.
Old roots are preserved while diverse ones are introduced.
Community is formed through bouquets of individual thought.
> *Trevor, summer volunteer*

Movies started in Culver City.
I like The Graduate
And I come to L.A. GOAL on weekends
To do Tai Chi with my mom on Fridays,

Art, drama and music on Saturdays,
And I go out with Molly to dinner, dessert and movies
Every Saturday evening.
She's my girlfriend.
I met Molly through my friend Jessica
30 years ago.
Molly lives in Culver City
With her parents,
And my girlfriend is the reason why
Culver City is important to me.

      Josh

What I like about Culver City
Is that I love it here at L.A. GOAL.
Before I came here
I made some really bad choices
In my life.
Since I've been here
I've learned to communicate
With my family — my mother, father, brother and three sisters —
Whenever I have a problem with them.

Probably the best thing for me
At L.A. GOAL
Is having learned to understand
And communicate
Appropriately
With others.

      Amin

Oh! L.A. GOAL, our beautiful facility,
Let me count the ways . . .
Meeting friends old and new,
It's like the glory days.
The paintings in the art room
Look so unique, like a sculpture made out of ice.
So many people, so little time.

Oops! Make sure you turn off your device.

I adore Culver City,
A city so neat,
Stores, eateries, and theatres too
And museums couldn't be beat.
There are coffee shops all around
This beautiful, wonderful place,
Even a pizzeria where
You can feed your face.

If there's one thing about the city,
One thing you should know—
You're so pretty!
>   *Dorian*

L.A. GOAL Poets by Sandra Coopersmith

My poets have spoken,
Their thoughts they've expressed,
And I am so happy
And truly impressed
Because when it comes to Culver City,
The feelings they share
Make it easy to see
How much they do care.

We celebrate our wonderful city!

Culver City Senior Center

Culver City Senior Center

BY AUDREY HESS

In 1972, the Culver City Senior Center opened
   across the street from where it is now in the old library.
After 25 years it moved to 4095 Overland and it is more contemporary.

They offer classes such as Zumba, Mahjong, Ukulele,
   Harmonica and Yiddish and others.
Some people hesitate to join and have their druthers.

On Sunday and Tuesday they show a movie,
Some are old and some are groovy.

Karaoke is on Tuesday morning and Wednesday afternoon.
They have patio barbeques starting in June.

In the hall they play Dominos and cards.
From the Teen Center to our current location is many yards.

It is $13.00 to join plus $5.00 to park.
When you arrive you have hit the mark.

Now you know when the center was created,
I found it on the internet so it can't be debated.

Shall We Dance?
BY MIRIAM SCHNEPP

Dancing is like dreaming with your feet
Body and soul respond to the beat
Of the music that sends you to secret places
That your heart so joyfully embraces

Prince Charming can whirl you around
As he takes his clue from the sound
It allows him to feel in control
As you both achieve your musical goal

How often does your heart and soul float free
And you can be anyone you want to be
He can let go of all worries and cares
And imagine himself as Fred Astaire
And you in turn Ginger Rogers can be
As you twirl around so gracefully

As the music lets you float on a cloud
As it comes your way both clear and loud
Allow it to help the world go by
Imagine yourself able to fly

Sometimes your feet misbehave
And don't listen to orders you gave
But the beauty of dreaming with your feet
Is that for the moment both of you meet.

Shake, Rattle 'n Roll

BY MO DE KOFF

They sway rhythmically as a pair,
   no need to think about each move.
Dancing partners without a care,
   gliding together in the "Groove."

They've both dressed very similar;
   they easily move fast or slow.
Rock band music's so familiar,
   It twirls them back to long ago.

She wears a Fifties' "poodle" skirt
   and has saddle shoes on her feet.
He's in pegged pants and crisp white shirt—
   shake, rattle 'n roll To The Beat!

The third Center's Senior Prom date,
   ends now with their favorite tune.
No worries 'bout being out late—
   it's just FOUR … in the *Afternoon*!

Sitting on the Senior Center Patio

BY MARSHA WILDE

Water splashes from a pipe
into the mini pool of the Senior Center
Palm fronds wave 'neath a lowering sky
    Why?

The wind blows on one side of me
The sun burns the other side
Ah, the ever-fascinating duality
    of California!

The rich, the poor
The ever so hardworking folk
The folk who have perhaps never worked
    and do not wish to work

The doers, the talkers
the dreamers
and the dreamed of
    today out here on the patio

At the Senior Center
on the only patio I know,
half the sky is blue
    half an increasingly darkening blue-gray

Shall I leave off my writing
and wend my way home? Or stay?
Keep feeling pleased, even happy —
    and perhaps, eventually, very very *wet* … ?

Oh! I am rooted to my solitary place here
And here will remain for a bit …..
Splat Splat Splat Splat *Splat* —
    Uh oh ---- !!!

The Patio
BY SHEILA STECKLER

Flags fluttering,
a cacaphony
of noises from
the crowd; mothers,
fathers, sweethearts,
children, toddlers
roaming on the grass,
sitting, eating, playing,
impatiently waiting
for the Irish music makers to begin!

Life
BY B.T. KHANH

How do we measure LIFE?
By the number of years lived
Or by the legacy it leaves behind?

LIFE is like a piece of Music,
With moments of Strength and Softness,
Tragedy and Cheerfulness.

LIFE is like a Garden of many Colors
Where Flowers bloom on fertile ground
And Butterflies dance to Happy Sounds.

LIFE is like a Poem,
Soothing, Healing, Taking a Stand
Rainbow of Hope over raging waterfall.

LIFE, above all, is Service and Kindness,
Unbeatable Spirit, unconditional Love,
Always shining through, as the true Measures of LIFE.

This, is a Tribute to LIFE
A Tribute to our Culver City Senior Center
The Heart of LIFE

Around Culver City

Oasis in the Heart of Los Angeles

BY B.T. KHANH

In Los Angeles, a few things are fairly constant :
heavy traffic on the 405
tourist clogged Hollywood Walk of Fame…
and an urban Oasis named Culver City !

Come ,
walk through its neighborhoods, quiet and
graced with eco landscaping ,
exchange a smile or two with its friendly residents.

Come,
relax in one of its many parks ,
watch them come alive in summertime
with children's laughs and Shakespeare's plays.

Come,
spend a day at the Community Garden
connect with people through plants and flowers
for sun, fun and healthy living.

Come,
ride along the La Ballona Creek,
be greeted with the colors of native plants
and inspiring mural art.

Come,
climb to the summit of Baldwin Hills,
admire the sight as the sun sets over the city,
stay for an evening concert under the stars.

Come,
blessed by Nature,
loved by those who called it Home,
Culver City is waiting for you.

Conjunctive Points Sonnet

BY ED ROSENTHAL

Each day we leave the strip that Harry Culver claimed
and cross Concrete Ballona at the L.A. border
At Turning Point School where I drop off my daughter
And there, you pop out like the particles of matter that physicists name

Curving steel that winks like sexy eye lashes;
Flying steps that climb outside the building's box,
hang out over the cars in the morning passage
and linger like steel flowers that intoxicate and entice

Because you are a mirror of nature's own ways,
your outside structures match your inside functions
When you say "Build To Suit", you're talking DNA
Combining beauty and utility in one construction
Form flows from function like flesh on bones

Culver City Sighting
BY RALPH THURSTON SEATON

Sunshine spot between cramped
Towns Rays smile on the future
Displays charms of the past

Paints now new beauty scenes
Honors the founder's hopes
With focused camera scopes

Culver City calls art without walls
Pictures life in movie sites Bakes
Classical and Jazz into airy nights

Where people enjoy nearby sea or strand
Under clouds slipping down from
Friendly hills above LA land

Where nature sat green trees
Architects built wonder And
Time changed most all to please

As many-to-come years shall show
An entire world can know This
Place draped in elegant lace.

Culver City, My Gem of a Place to Live
BY ANN GARRETT

At the Culver City Senior Center
I love the singing, dancing, musical instrument instructions
all the parties with musicians and decorations and good food
I love the movies every week, sometimes twice a week
the instructors are an inspiration with my favorite class the Poetry Group
led by Dr. Janet Hoult, the Honorary Poet Laureate of Culver City
and our inspired, kind leader.

It is here in this Center that I am witness to human beings
their hearts lifted up, their eyes and lips smiling, their hands
reaching out to shake my hand, and then sometimes hugging me
I go to the lunches where I meet very interesting people
some have had strokes or major physical issues
but their personalities shine through
I recognize many members by name
so glad we are all alive each day.

Yet, there is another kindness I have found in Culver City
it is with the police, the men and women
and especially one day when going to Ralphs Grocery on Jefferson Avenue
a woman near the closed recycle center was very upset, yelling loudly
she was dragging a heavy black plastic bag needing to recycle bottles, cans
but it was a holiday and there were no staff and no money for food, for dinner
the woman then dragged her bag into Ralphs
making herself known, yelling, cursing.
A security guard escorted her outside with great kindness
where I decided to go up to her holding up a $20 bill
she hesitated and then came over to me
I gave her $25 for dinner and breakfast
this woman began to cry saying she needed money for food
and forgot the recycling center would be closed, forgot the holiday
just then a Culver City police car came up
and I told them I was a social worker and discerned what might have happened.
"This is my angel who gave me money to eat"
I heard the woman say to the policemen

a policeman came up and told me I was a very kind angel
and said they knew the woman well and that she needs help
I turned to the woman and told her I knew the policemen would be kind to her
and that she should also be kind to them
she nodded yes and then said they were always kind to her
and now in Culver City, I have found my gem of a small city.

The Culver Hotel

BY AUDREY HESS

The Culver Hotel was built in 1924
Harry Culver's offices occupied the first and second floor.
In 1938 the little people AKA the Munchkins stayed there during the filming of
The Wizard of Oz
Charlie Chaplin, John Wayne and Red Skelton have all been the Boz (boss)

Over the next few decades the property fell in disrepair,
It was boarded up in the nineteen-eighties and nobody could stay there.
In the 1990s it got demolished
It was partially reopened and polished.

The hotel changed hands after a hotelier bought the hotel in 2007
Since then the plumbing and electrical were done, which was heaven
They kept the hotel's architectural integrity,
The hotel has been one of LA's go-to venues for nightly jazz
    and more around the city.

It is neighbors with Culver Studios
And a few blocks from Metro-Goldwyn-Mayer, now Sony,
Which is across the street from the Culver City Senior Center
    which is a diddy

To this day they still film the hotel inside and out—
It was a street in London, an apartment in Barcelona,
    or a café in Paris, and other places.
Some celebrities stayed there such as Clark Gable, Mickey Rooney,
Frank Sinatra and other faces.
Dwight D. Eisenhower even had a campaign office in 1952
I have been there. Have you?

I Choose to Chew Chewy Cheese
BY LESLIE LENELL

I choose to chew chewy cheese.
Please give me two pounds to eat with ease.
It can be chopped, chunky, diced, sliced, grated:
I'll be overjoyed, even elated.
Mouth-watering melted mozzarella mounds;
Eating lots of cheese 'til I'm a balloon inflated.

"Chewy Cheese" can be found in the many wonderful restaurants and markets
in Culver City..!

Rain, Rain / Culver City
BY EDITH GOODMAN

Rain/Rain

The rain finally came and what a pain.
Streets are wet lines, that you cannot see
Trucks and SUVs go faster
Than cars as before,
So the best thing to do
Is to stay home!

Culver City

The trains and buses go by.
   to give you a safe ride
Culver City has many to take
   you where you want to go
Either shopping, eating or
   the Ocean to watch the waves go by
Walking the Boardwalk in the sun
   will also keep you hot and dry

Culver City Alive

BY RUTH BERMAN

Culver City is governed so well
From the schools to the pools to the Culver Hotel
There's so much to tell that rings the bell

Like the parks where wee children come to play
They have so much fun there, day after day

The theatres, restaurants and neat tree-lined streets
And the trendy place to buy special treats

The Fire and Police Departments so efficiently run
If an accident happens, how swiftly they come

For senior citizens and others in need
Help arrives quickly, yes indeed

So come, smell the flowers as Spring springs alive
For Culver City is a great place
    to love, live and thrive

Culver City Parks / Nature

Bandits in the Night

BY ALICE GARDELLO

Tripping the sensor light in my neighbor's backyard
Traversing my patio roof top
I can hear their claws grasping the trunk as they go
Shimmying down the pine tree.

Disturbing my peaceful and needed slumber
I spy four raccoons, one-at-a-time, playing follow the leader.
Ruthless critters, who travel in packs
Marauders in the night.

Ripping off tree branches and stealing my nearly ripe fruit.
Pillaging my fuyu persimmon tree
How ruthless and callow they are
Nasty and rough.

I know they need food to survive.
But, I am angered by their rude and aggressive manner.
My backyard is not a playground to be ransacked.
These trespassers are not welcome!

These bandits in the night—with no regard for a person's property..
They must be stopped!

Veterans Park and Auditorium

BY JOANNE WOLF

Veterans Park is a wonderful park.
It's approximately one long block square,
And what makes it so amazing
Are the happenings one finds there.

It has a picnic area
Near the swings, slides and climbing toys
And a sand area where the children play
While the parents watch their joy.

Many birthdays and celebrations are held here
For everyone from young to old
As families and friends come for parties and games
And enjoy as the activities unfold.

The park has areas to play all kinds of ball
In which so many people take part.
There's tennis, basketball, baseball and soccer.
They all watch or take part as games start.

The park is great to walk in
Or to jog in if that is your joy
And this is beneficial to your life
Whether you're man, woman, girl or boy.

It's a place for big celebrations.
City Fiestas are often held here.
It's a place where Races can start or end
It's busy throughout the whole year.

People come to the park to enjoy themselves
And share events with the whole Community.
Events that are planned to be fun and fulfilling
Planned with utmost care and ingenuity.

The Park also has a Swimming Pool
With lessons and contests and fun
The High School also uses the pool
It's great with the days in the sun.

The Veterans Park Auditorium and building
Is a landmark for Community Events.
Its rooms house the meetings for all kinds of groups
That appeal to both ladies and gents.

It has a special Teen Center
That helps Teens grow and thrive
By offering activities and field trips
That aid and enrich their lives.

The Auditorium holds Services for different Religions
It has Expos for all to attend.
It has classes that many people enjoy
So many activities the city does commend.

During the Holidays, the tower is lit up
With lights that are seen far and wide
So everyone can see and be aware
Of Culver City lit up with pride.

The Auditorium periodically holds Concerts
For the enjoyment of all Music lovers.
It sometimes has voting or indoor sports games
And projects in which one can discover

How to grow your plants by the Garden Club
Or how to improve in some skills.
One can exercise, sing or do many more things
And they all add to life with thrills.

So this is a park that is widely used
By so many people-whether a few or a crowd.
It's a part of the lives of the people who live here
And a Park of which our City is proud.

Lindberg Park

BY ALICE GARDELLO

Annual Fourth of July parade and lively block party.
"Pickfest" to close the school year.
Circular cul-de-sac
Bounded by the Ballona Creek and Jefferson Blvd.

Park with children playing and laughing
Birthday parties on the weekend
Rousing soccer and softball games
Families, children, teenagers and seniors all together

Professionals, educated graduates
A sense of community
Responsible citizens
Model Neighborhood Watch Program
A Realtor's delight!

People walking dogs
Joggers, walkers and babies in strollers
Friendly neighbors, who know my name
And I know theirs

Peace and quiet at night and during the day
Xerscape gardens and well-manicured lawns
Tall, aging trees,
Blooming flowers and verdant shrubbery.

That's why I like Lindberg Park — A sparkling gem of Culver City
And a place that I call home.

Culver City—Baldwin Park

BY NORMA GLICKMAN

There's a beautiful park at the crest of a hill
Overlooking the whole city —
Where the air is freshened by a breeze
That sometimes warms and
Sometimes chills. On a smoggy day
The ocean reflects a dun colored haze
That hovers like a soiled blanket
Along the length of the shoreline — and
Downtown disappears — but

On a clear day — the song about seeing forever
Rises spontaneously to my lips as I trace the horizon
From Sony Studios at my feet, and Culver City
Spread out like a scale-model diorama
Below the Santa Monica mountains

I never tire of scanning the 170 degree panorama
Stretching the length of the Pacific coastline —
North to Malibu — south to Catalina
Snow-capped Mt. Baldy to the east
The long, sandy beach from Playa del Rey
Almost to Downtown Los Angeles,
Santa Monica, Beverly Hills, the Hollywood sign,
Griffith Park, the Getty Museum and the
Snake-like Santa Monica Freeway

Leaning against the guard rail
I overlook this perfect, miniature world,
And wish it was possible that its pristine beauty
Could filter the dross and the hatreds and the imperfections
That dwell beneath those miniature rooftops
Overarched by this "blue true dream of sky."

Two Faces of La Ballona

BY STEVEN GELB

I went with my friend, Marie,
One Friday night, to see,
The La Ballona Festival.
We viewed its two Faces:
One, Fast Asleep;
The other, Wide Awake.
Their differences, just as stark,
As light proceeds from dark.
I now will share with you,
Impressions of the two:

The Sleeping Face we saw,
Not open, had some flaws:
The pizza stand smells without wares,
The music tent is silent and alone,
The Ferris Wheel is gigantic, but deserted.
La Ballona waits in the wings,
For many different things.
Whatever will bring it to life?
I toot on a phantom pipe!

The sound of the pipe was key,
Our Festival now to see!
The pizza stand peddles its goods,
The music tent rocks with a beat,
The Ferris Wheel turns round and around.
La Ballona jumps awake,
Its purpose now to make,
An experience for us all,
And we will have a ball!

La Ballona's two Faces,
Present many traces:
Asleep before waking,
Then vibrantly Alive.

We feast on the food,
We sway to the beat,
We thrill on the rides.
But it's time for the fun to end,
Our memories now to tend!
To all our friends, far and near,
We must wait until next year!

California Autumn

BY SHEILA STECKLER

Curled, dried leaves
Skitter across the pavement
Rusty shards drift slowly to earth
A merciless Southern sun beats down
On thirsty, parched earth!

Culver City Activities

Screenland 5K—Centennial Run

BY ANGIE WALLER

Dripping grey skies
Could not dampen
The enthusiasm
Of Sunday's 5K racers,
Whether bundled up
Against the cold and damp
Or bedecked in costume
Young and old, and in between,
Some 3500 ran or sauntered along
Culver City's downtown streets:

There were witches in black,
Cone-shaped hats and flowing skirts,
A Dorothy with Toto excitedly trotting
Along beside her,
A man pushed an infant in a stroller with yellow-brick road
Attached and there were
Lions and Tin Men, Scarecrows and Munchkins
All mingled with the crowds
Shuffling through the studio
Under the rainbow which soared
Brightly against the sunless sky.

Music live and taped
Kept spirits light along the way
It was indeed a day to
Sing and dance in the rain.
Then finally the finish line
A photo op and Medal earned
A sense of accomplishment
And celebration.
So what if there was no sun?
The run (or walk) was still fun.

Biking Ballona
BY ELIZABETH HARRIS

The feel of the wind against my cheeks
As I bike down the Ballona Creek
No cars in the street
Only riders and joggers to meet

Burning off calories
As I work that pedal
On those uphill climbs
How sublime!
Am I skinny yet?

Egrets, seagulls, and ducks
Perhaps a white heron or two
I stop and grab a shot with my phone
Capturing the magic so close to home
Nature at its best
On this beautiful day of rest

I stop and watch
The motion of the ocean
As I hit the beach
It's a grasp within my reach
I turn back for home
Grateful for the wind against my cheeks
Biking back up the Ballona Creek.

Swim, Swam, Swum

BY MO DE KOFF

Yah, yah, yah,yah. We swim! We swam. We swum...
Each mornin' by Nine — we've taken the plunge.
Where? You ask? Why at the Plunge, don'tcha know?
The Culver City Municipal Pool
Whether heatwave or dome, we keep our cool.

Drive on Overland — that's us a-bobbin'
Up and down in turquoise clear blue water,
Weather buoys, no matter the weather,
We are the Plungers a-keepin' our cool —
At Culver City's Municipal Pool.

With our teachers: Sandy, Kim and Nancy —
We do "crabby squats" movin' like big crabs;
We climb the wall, do vertical pushups.
We swing our legs like pendulums, point toes
We stand straight, leg's a hinge, open 'n' close.

We exercise to lose our "Grandma" arms —
We run in place, punchin' the water, then
We hurry to get our favorite noodle ...
We do some "bunny hops," 'n "rockin' horse;"
We shake to the "hokey pokey," of course.

We invent names, like "happy baby feet"
And "Froggy" bicycle's on our noodles.
And "thigh master" "Scissor legs" — right and left
And "leg crunches" "Jumpin' Jacks" and "Low Jack"
Use your noodle: on your heels, stretch your back

Yah, yah, yah, yah. We swim! We swam. We swum...
We marched! Didcha see us in the Parade?
We twirled noodles down Culver Boulevard!
We wore Plungers caps in black and lime green!
Were you there, hmm? Well then, ya musta seen!

We're easy to spot, having so much fun.
We exercise hard — and we laugh, laugh and love
The Culver City Municipal Pool
We plunge right into the sparklin' water.
We hope you'll join us. You really *otter*!!

Plunge Picnic in Haiku
BY MO DE KOFF

Carlson Park picnic—
Plungers' potluck summer lunch;
No swimsuits, just clothes!

Shakespeare in the Park

BY ANGIE WALLER

Wither goest thou today?
—Carlson Park to see a play
"As You Like It", a romance
Join me if you have the chance.

Branches arching from a tree
Form a shady canopy,
There beneath a stage is set
Where the actors are well met
Whether in the forest Arden
Or yet Oliver's fruit garden
Or it be the Duke's domain
We are drawn in just the same
Carried by the actor's craft
Willingly we play our part.

"All the world's a stage" they say
In Carlson Park it was today.

Culver City's Fiesta

BY MICHAEL POIZNER

The City's Fiesta La Ballona
has long been a City annual event.
With great anticipation I look forward to
sampling the many different delicious foods.

The rhythmic music and dancing
are always very entertaining.
Browsing the many business and
organizational booths can be both
interesting and educational.

The squeals of delight piercing the air
from the children on the carnival rides,
The pony rides and Petting Zoo, all busy
with the kids awaiting their turn.

Usually running into friends and neighbors,
It feels like one big community get-together.
I can't wait until it's Fiesta time next year.

Fiesta La Ballona

BY ANGIE WALLER

The warm air pulses
With the thrumming hum of trucks
Arrayed around the backs
Of myriad carnival rides—
Twirling, turning,
Stomach-churning—
Rides from which
The screams and giggles
Of giddy riders emanate.
Rows of booths entice
With crafted goods and games,
And from the food stalls
Greasy, salty smells
Assault the noses
Of fiesta visitors swarming by—
Popcorn and chicken,
Chili, nachos, cheese dogs.
A bevy of bands produces
A mosaic of music;
Dancers twirl and swirl or slide and glide;
And stilted ladies in sumptuous costumes
Strut and sway in time.
The sun slips from the sky
But the fiesta fun lingers into the night.

A Perfect City

BY HELEN SEID

Down Overland to Westfield Mall
Culver City has it all,
Quiet streets and parks galore
No other city gives you more.

If north and south you need to go
The 405 may be too slow,
So take Sepulveda where you will see
What a perfect city is meant to be,
Where homes and stores sit side by side
Next to the busy four-o-five

And if you travel east to west
Washington Blvd. is the best
From end to end and thru downtown
Culver City wins the crown.
With restaurants and a historic hotel
This is the place you'll want to dwell.

Our Police and Fire can't be outdone
And all our schools are number one.
With a senior center and one for teens
Check out our Dog Park by all means

The Plunge, Vet's Aud, and museums too
There's certainly plenty for all to do.
Our Synagogue, Churches and Mosque provide
A place for all to worship with pride.

With all of this it's plain to see
Why the Heart of Screenland is the place for me.

The Heart of Screenland

The Heart of Screenland

BY ANGIE WALLER

Now close your eyes
Let the memories rise —
Of a giant ape
Causing viewers to gape,
How Munchkins strode
Down a yellow brick road,
An inferno soared
For the lion that roared,
When dance and song
Moved the stories along.
Magic took place
In dusty open space
For the city's heart
Comes from film-land's start
H. Culver's plan
Built The Heart of Screenland.

A Tribute to Hal Roach Studio

BY LINDA CHILDS

Our Culver City
Had a movie studio
That gave us laughter.

Scene: Culver City; Take: 100

BY SANDRA COOPERSMITH

Movies were my childhood magic carpet,
    wrapping me in memories that are sweet
And now I live in Culver City, just a few blocks down the street
From Sony Pictures Studios! The Heart of Screenland motto on our city seal
Adds, for this lifelong film addict, a lot more than a just dash of surreal
And living in this environment enhances that sensation,
Our film history inspiring me in this poetic celebration.

Long before the "talkies" our founder, Harry Culver, spotted Thomas Ince, a
    famous film maker
Who was shooting a Western on Ballona Creek, so Mr. Culver, a real mover
    and shaker
Persuaded him to transfer his studio operations to a local site
On Washington Boulevard, and he was so right
Because in 1915 Ince/Triangle Studios was built in the town that later
    became
The Heart of Screenland, movies being a major factor in our claim to fame,
Clearly tracing back to Mr. Culver's prophetic foresight
And oh, by the way,
After later housing film makers including MGM, that's where Sony Pictures
    Studios stands today.

I honor our visionary founder, for it is because
Of his dream that we saw Judy Garland in the Wizard of Oz.
The huge rainbow installed on Sony's grounds brings memories galore
Of that incredible film, and it's just one production out of so many more.
Remember the Tin Man singing "If I Only Had a Brain"?
Remember Gene Kelly dancing in Singin' in the Rain?
Ever see Grand Hotel? Dinner at Eight? Andy Hardy? Quo Vadis?
Mrs. Miniver? Silk Stockings? Dr, Kildare? An American in Paris?
These are but a handful, a miniscule few
Of the memorable movies MGM managed to do.
The list goes on and on, containing favorites we all hold dear,
So as we celebrate The Heart of Screenland's Centennial year,
Let's thank Harry Culver for his magical seeds that grew
Into a splendid world of cinema for me and all of you.

Under the Lights
BY JESSICA BURNETT

Sitting center
Surrounded by earth
We dreamt
Dreamt of creating sustenance
Breathing life and spirit into
Dreams

Lighting candles in crevices unseen
We gave birth
To rain-bowed people
Hues highlighting the skies
Peace, kissed on each of their faces
Babies crawled around the lips of storytellers
Drifted into sleep under large trees
Diving into blue waters cradled by the cheers of families and friends

We have seen courage
Spread its wings in our heart
Dancing in between dinners
Collecting among pulsing memories

This city.. Like a phoenix
Falls to pieces and rises
And those who remember
Tell tales over ice cream
And Carnival rides

We appreciate you Culver
And we wear your stamp
Knowing you have knit us into one.

Magical Movies

BY RUTH BERMAN

When I was just a child of nine
Mum gave me money
To go to the Saturday matinee
Which cost just a dime
The movie house was not far away
I knew I would sit and stay there all day.

My eyes were joyfully glued to the screen
With such intensity, I lived in every scene
The projector started shining its lights
Then the magic began
First there were short subjects
That was the plan
A serial, a cartoon, news and much more
And with much anticipation on came the magical score
The heavy satin drapes would then part
Which meant the main feature would soon start.

How exciting that was
Not a sound could be hard
Not even a buzz!
Too many to mention… so many titles
There sure was an abundance of matinee idols
They came in all sizes — big and small
From Cagney and Bogart to Lauren Bacall
I fell in love with Clark Gable with all of my heart
"It Happened One Night".. that was the start!
I knew when I grew up I'd be able to marry
A man just like Clark Gable
And I did….

Movie Memories
BY JOANNE WOLF

There are many people, some older and gray
Whose heart's have a part that still wants to play,
And the movies of Disney we saw long ago
We remember as awesome in a wonderful way.

Cinderella was beautiful and sweet while she cleaned.
Her step-sisters and step-mom were nasty and mean.
When Prince Charming found her and the shoe fit just right,
We were all overjoyed and filled with delight.

Bambi was precious, his friends were great too.
Flower and Thumper were cute, loyal and true.
When Bambi's mom died, we cried in deep sadness
But Bambi's dad came and made sense of the madness.

Snow White was a beauty like a beautiful jewel,
But her villainous step-mom was bad, mean and cruel.
Snow White ate from the apple, went into deep sleep,
But then the Prince came and kissed her and we didn't have to weep.

So many marvels on Screens through the years,
Some movies brought laughs, others sadness and tears.
But the enjoyment has filled us with memories divine
Culver City's Studios are really so fine.

Thank you for the memories we'll never forget,
For youngsters and oldsters, the fantasies still are met.
So for ladies and gentlemen, for girls and for boys,
The movies still bring us continuous joys!

Thank You, Culver City.

Dreaming Upon a Rainbow

BY B.T. KHANH

Inspired by "The Wizard of Oz"

...*"Somewhere, over the rainbow, skies are blue*
And the dreams that you dare to dream really do come true"...
(Harburg, E Y / Arlen, Harold)

Dare we dream that some day
World Leaders'd meet and walk down the Yellow Brick Road
in quest of a Heart, a Brain , and a "Nerve" ?

...*"I'd be tender, I'd be gentle...*
I'd be friend with the sparrows ... If I only had a heart ".

Dare we dream of a World where Sparrows of all breeds'd
play and zip through serene skies ? ...then ride the rainbow home ,
to that Magic Land where troubles melt into harmony
as the music plays on?

"I'd unravel every riddle
For any individ'al In trouble or in pain ...If I only had a brain "

Dare we dream of a Health Care System
Efficient and Compassionate ,
for everyone in need, Body and Soul ?

"Though my tail would lash, I would show compash
For every underling... If I-If I were King !

Dare we dream that some day
World Leaders'd speak words of Truth and Wisdom ,
and conflicts,'d be resolved
with less of a "lash" and more of a "compash" ?
Dare we dream ?....

I Live in Oz
BY ELIZABETH HARRIS

Somewhere over the rainbow
Is here and now
I walk down the street after a quick stop at the Jackson Market,
Taking in the glow of the multi-colored arch
Rising out of Sony's gate
The Emerald City is alive and well outside my doorstep
Steeped in movie history
Hail Dorothy and Toto too.
Flying monkeys, wizards that aren't
A wise scarecrow who can't scare a sparrow
A sentimental tin man in need of an artificial heart
On his way to Southern California Hospital bumps into
Cowardly lion, bravest of the brave, maybe not, but what a roar
Like my dog, Jack, who's scared of a tack, but can bark with the best of 'em.
Did you happen to see Glinda glide over the Culver Hotel in a bubble?
I did, and the wicked witch was there, too, lurking around the ArcLight,
Reminding me of the nightmares she gave me as a child.
And here I am living in the same town as she!
Heading over to Grand Casino on Main Street for the American breakfast,
I stop, look around and pinch myself.
My favorite movie has come to life, and I can honestly say,
"There's No Place Like Home," Culver City!

Culver City Thoughts

A Valentine for Culver City

BY JOANNE WOLF

Culver City, you're a special place
Here's a Valentine to you.
You provide much for all of us
Who live here — things to do.

We have a Senior Center
With many activities and classes,
Many clubs and groups do meet there.
It's filled up with the masses.

It even has a work-out gym
To keep the seniors fit.
And it has dances and big events
That make this place a hit.

No matter what your interest
You'll probably find it there,
Because activities vary
Throughout the entire year.

Carnivals, races, college and schools
Culver City even has a mall.
Parks, pools and the Veterans' Aud
It really has it all.

So Culver City, You are great
You have so much to give,
And we who are here all agree
This is a great place to live.

Happy Valentine's Day Culver City

The More Things Change, The More They Stay the Same

BY TERESA RASCHILLA

Every year, eight kids lined up to take a back-to-school photo
  in front of the palm tree at the end of the driveway on Hannum Avenue.
EIGHT kids!
Three decades of smiling (and not smiling) in front of that tree.
How did my grandparents do it?
I arrived a generation later:
Age 5, beaming gap-toothed in nervous anticipation.
First stop: Palm Tree Paparazzi.
Then? Parading down Sawtelle, an entourage of aunts and uncles in tow.

Mac, the Crossing Guard, Mrs. Kelly's Kindergarten Class.
Uncle Irv, reading to us on the mat.
Red Light, Red Light, what do you say?
Round-nosed scissors, enormous crayons, and that very particular smell of paste.

Every year began with a photo.
"C'mon Teresa. Okay, Adam get in there. Stop making those faces, you two!
Just Adam now…" Good thing film was much cheaper then.

My mom had Ms. Hoffman…I had her as Mrs. May.
Aunt Dicka had gone to school with Principal Fox.
Mr. Pete took over and promised to put the Pal in Princi-Pal,
  stomping around in huge furry slippers.
I ran for student council and sang in chorus.
Adam won a ribbon at the Science Fair.
On his first day at El Rincon, he'd heard a thousand times about his "family
  legacy"
It didn't phase him. It probably didn't even register.

All my son knew was I was making him stand, ridiculously,
  in front of a palm tree in front of my parents' house,
  while he was instructed to "Smile!"
"Open your eyes!" "Look natural."
"Don't give me that face!"
"Gosh I love you" by his mom…and grandma…and great-aunt…and
  great-grandma…
Thank goodness for digital cameras.

A Celebration of the Future

BY HELEN SEID

As I sat in my big easy chair last night
I thought of the city with great delight
For our Bicentennial all our history will be told
As we celebrate Culver City's 200 years old

My neighbor is from Mars, you know
We get along just great
There is no longer prejudice, animosity or hate.

My robots clean and cook and shop
Their work is just the best
Since I don't need to do those things
I put my feet up and rest.

When I need a car, I call it and when it comes it's free
Each person gets a flying car that offers privacy.
It takes me to the doctor, to the market or the store
And flies away to wait for me since we don't drive on streets anymore.

The big earthquake came a few years ago
It was very sad to see
But since that time Culver City
Has become beachfront property.

Our mayor, Jim Clarke IV, represents the city
And the citizens he has inspired
And that is why he makes us proud
And he is so admired

Then suddenly I awake and find things aren't what they may seem
And it's only two thousand and seventeen
And as for the changes, what more do I find
That I've dreamt all of this and it's all in my mind.

nighthawk

BY CHRIS KAY NORTHRUP

It is 3 a.m. on culver boulevard riding west
through LA's bifurcated Ballona wetlands
streaming toward the salted sea.

Quiet overwhelms the dark
inked outline of the Santa Monica Mountains in the distance
pitch black silhouette of palms scattered under a sliver of a recumbent moon.

Whisper of the ancient Tongva people rises from the reeds
and trickling stream a white heron taking flight
at the dead center of LA's antediluvian calm.

When 10 million people have gone away
and you breathe in what might have been
…before the break of day.

Culver City Sci-Fi

BY DAVID KATZ

Oh my
I'm living in the Culver City Main Street pod
New store offers neurolinguistic interpretation
of electrical data
it's a new chip in my head
The mayor of Culver City
wants to replace the artificial food center
to a more modernized update
The plastic force of protons and electrons that are the protector
of the Culver Dome
need to be replaced
Food fields 5 Virginia Ave. are so tall now 75 stories high love
the different colors
want to take a tour
I'm at Jefferson the bionic parts store just opened up a
new sales lead
I'm wondering if I should apply
Oh my
they have this new record
store old record store
I wonder wow the view
it is it seems like people are moving their arms and legs and going up and down
I hear weird sounds like cha-cha
Must be some strange antiquated Culver City ritual
The Culver City chamber of commerce wants to incorporate a no-fly zone over
my living dwelling place
What's the difference the robots fly around in my head sprinkling new
information anyway

The Culver City Schools
are some of the best, the technology inside the brain centers is so amazing
our children love to sing perhaps they will teach them to laugh as well!

It's kind of laughable
At senior citizen center

It's closed now
No one gets old anymore
Though personally I sometimes think
It would be interesting
To find out what it's like
to be old
Where is that movie library lot
Where you see images of people with wrinkles on their face
How strange is that!
Oh my
They just opened the time capsule Ralphs
How weird it looks like paper box with poetry on them
Black ink words
Wow
Oh my
Look at this weird picture of somebody eating
Food
How primitive can you get
Looking at Overland
Avenue
They used to drive metal cars
Hold it hold it
Google is redoing my Culver City circuits
Oh my that feels good
My memory was kind of getting old
Maybe that's what
they mean by old
I'm told
Oh my
Like living here
Of course I've never been out of
Culver City
Why bother
Need to say goodbye
What a great place this says
Love Culver City
Just love it

Culver City Here I Come

BY RUTH BERMAN

Are you a different nation?
I hear you speak with such loyalty and admiration

Tell me, do I need a passport to enter your fair city?
Do you speak the same language as I do?
Do you have your own national anthem?

The pride you share from all who live here
Makes me want to pack up and move…where…?

CULVER CITY

My best friend lives here, I visit all the time
Fun, parties and toasting with fine wine
Fourth of July fireworks in accordance with the law
We stand there watching with excitement and awe

Not to forget the "Overland Café" where once a week we meet
To talk and to share the delicious food we eat
Oh.. and I must tell you that is where I met
Culver City's Poet Laureate…Dr. Janet

Block parties, dancing, barbeques galore
Living in Culver City can never be a bore
The Senior Citizen's Center is the best in the West
And I do so love the Culver City Crest

Should I move or should I not
Living in Beverly Hills is not so hot…!

Culver City Acrostic

BY ROSALIE KIRSCH

C ulver City's origin and history
U sually
L ovingly
V ery
E nthusiastically
R ecited, repeated and reiterated

C onstantly
I nterestingly
T oday
Y early, and on every occasion!

The End of Our Centennial Year

BY DR. JANET HOULT

We've had our Centennial Celebration
It had to be one of the best in the nation
Events were planned that were large and small
To ensure that fun could be had by all
A parade, birthday party, contests and Fiesta
The Centennial Committee had no time for siestas..!

Now that we look to the future once more
We have memories racked up by the score

When our time capsule's opened in 2117
Will our great-grandkids understand what it means?
Will they, like us, look back on the past
With a bicentennial celebration sure to be a blast..!
Of course they'll remember, it's never too late
To celebrate what makes Culver City great..!

Congratulations to all who participated and to all who made it happen.

Centennial Poetry Readings and Contest Awards

First Place — Helen Seid — "They Aren't Here Anymore"
The poem takes us on a trip through the years as she remembers what used to be here in Culver City and reminds us that our memories of what was there will continue to be with us.

Second Place — Ann Garrett — "My Gem of a Place to Live"
Ann moved here from Chicago and she shares her feelings about how special Culver City, our Senior Center and our Culver City Police Department are for her.

Third Place — Miriam Schnepp — "Shall We Dance"
"Poet in Residence" at the Senior Center, her lovely poem provides us with a sense of the joy our senior citizens share when they are involved in activities at the Senior Center.

Fourth Place — Audrey Hess — "The Culver Hotel"
Audrey's poem gives us the history and also some insights into one of Culver City's most historic buildings.

Judge: Lynne Bronstein is the author of four poetry collections, *Astray from Normalcy*, *Roughage*, *Thirsty in the Ocean*, and *Border Crossings*. Her poetry and short fiction have been published in magazines, newspapers, anthologies, and on web sites, including *Playgirl*, *Beyond Baroque Obras*, *California State Poetry Quarterly*, *VolNo*, *Electrum*, *Poetry Superhighway*, *poeticdiversity*, *Silver Birch Press*, *Chiron Review*, *Galway Review*, *Lummox*, *Spectrum*, *Voices from Leimert Park*, *The Art of Being Human*, *Revolutionary Poets Brigade*, *Free Venice Beachhead*, *Caffeine*, *OnTarget*, *Subtletea*, *The Stone Bird*, and *Al-Khemia*. In addition, she has been a journalist for five decades, writing for the *Los Angeles Times* and other Los Angeles area newspapers. She has been nominated for two Pushcart Prizes for poetry and for two Best of the Net Awards for short fiction. She won a prize for her short story "Why Me" and two prizes from Channel 37 public access for news writing. She has taught poetry and journalism workshops for children at 826LA and for the Arcadia Library and was cited by the city and county of Los Angeles for her mentoring work with Jewish Vocational Service.

About the Poets Who Contributed to the Centennial Collection

Ruth Berman is from Philadelphia, After she and her husband were married, they drove across the country and settled in Los Angeles where they have raised four kids. She has a degree in early childhood education with a specialization in autism. She has written poetry for her family and special occasions for many years, but this is the first time she has participated in poetry readings.

Linda Childs has lived in Culver City for thirty-one years and is retired from Culver City Unified School District. She is the mother of a twenty-six year old daughter and has a six year old granddaughter.

Ron Cohen was born in Cairo, raised in Israel and educated in the U.S. He has a B.A. and an M.A. in literature from UCLA and was the Bible champion of Los Angeles in 1971. Ron has published poetry in Hebrew and English in various publications and is the author of "The Talking Oak Tree" and "Mastering the Hebrew Language in 10 Easy Lessons". In June 2016 he retired after 47 years of teaching.

In her first life, **Sandra Coopersmith** was Senior VP of a commercial mortgage banking company, closing multimillion dollar real estate loans. In her spare time she created cartoons that she sold to several publications. Following retirement she became a journalist and is currently Features Writer for the Culver City Observer. Her volunteer activities include teaching poetry at L.A. GOAL to adults with developmental disabilities.

Mo de Koff was born and raised in Culver City. She's been writing poetry since she was a student at Betsy Ross Elementary School. Several of her earliest poems were printed in Culver High School anthologies and Girl Scout magazines. She has three grown sons and is active in the field of special needs.

Terry Anne Dicks is a retired School Principal and spent five years as a Religious Educator and Assistant Pastor. She began writing poetry only in the last couple of years because it seemed like a short form that gets her emotions on paper.

Alice Gardello, in spring 2016, placed third in the poetry category for the Marina District Women's Clubs, representing Culver City with her poem titled "Monteverde, Costa Rica". She retired as an educator from the LAUSD in June 2015 after 35 years of service and joined our poetry class in July 2015.

Ann Garrett is a retired VA Hospital Social Worker who loves taking trips along highway 101 and into mountains. Ann began writing off and on years ago and now plans to sit down daily to write.

Steven Gelb was born in Los Angeles and attended Los Angeles public schools. He received a Bachelor's degree in physics and a Master's degree in medical physics from UCLA. He was employed as a computer analyst at Hughes Aircraft and Boeing The author of many technical papers in the field of computer analysis, he has also written compositions and poems on topics such as space exploration.

Norma Glickman was born in London and grew up there during World War II. She came to Los Angeles in 1960 and discovered the joys of poetry about 10 years ago.

Edith Goodman lives in both Culver City and Los Angeles…referred to as Culver City adjacent.. Her work experience was in banking, bonds, bookkeeping and dormant accounts.

Pat Harmon has lived in Culver City for 18 years, but it wasn't until retirement that she was aware of the fact she wasn't just on the "west side of town". She is retired from both UCLA and USC and if she cared about football it would be a conflict. She was a project manager for genetic epidemiology studies for 30 years, by far her longest career even though she started as a social worker.

Elizabeth Harris is an actress, writer, and producer, in no certain order……who recently finished a short film, "Nothing as it Seems"…..and is the author of the book, "Little Fish in a Big Pond – A Support Guide for Actors".

Audrey Hess, who started writing poetry in the 4th grade, collects the peace sign and her favorite color is purple. She has a business called Audrey's Computer Tutor Service, where she assists people in learning how to use their computers, cellphones, tablets, laptops and more.

David Katz is an artist, a poet and a writer.

B.T. Khanh – Dr. Khanh, a nephrologist, likes to explore new interests, and wishes to thank the CC Senior Center for giving her the opportunity to explore and discover the beauty and creativity of Poetry.

Rosalie Kirsch is taking this class just to learn about poetry. She had never even thought about trying to write it…

L.A. GOAL was founded in 1969 as a private non-profit agency by parents of young adults with developmental disabilities, **L.A. GOAL** encourages its members to develop their personal abilities and strengths in a nurturing and supportive environment, thus raising their self-esteem and independent capabilities through a wide variety of programs including visual arts, sewing, music, drama, clinical services, counseling, vocational training, physical fitness, and social interaction. For more information visit lagoal.org. Petite Konstantin, Executive Director.

Leslie L. Lenell was born and raised in a suburb of Chicago called Lincolnwood. She has lived in Culver City for 20 years. She is a retired 2nd grade teacher from Los Angeles Unified School District.

Chris Kay Northrup — A publicist by trade and Culver City resident, Chris has been a broadcast reporter, news writer, film editor, director and documentary producer, and professor of journalism at Cal State Long Beach. She and her husband Bernie Roswig founded Culver City-based BJR Public Relations in 1978.

Michael Poizner is a Culver City resident. He is a retired employee of the City of Los Angeles and came to Culver City to join Joanne Wolf as her partner. He has been active in the Culver City Senior Center since its opening.

Teresa Bernadette Raschilla is an artist, writer, and third-generation Culver City resident. She has always delighted in the city's unique intersection of creative expression, scientific curiosity, multicultural celebration, technological advancement, and small-town heart.

Ed Rosenthal, Poet/Broker of Downtown Los Angeles, was known for successfully integrating his writing and real estate. He presented real estate issues in classical verse as his concerns ran from social justice issues to the practicality of closing deals. Not only did the Wall Street Journal publish a series of his rhyming couplets, Ed was the only poet to be published in the prestigious Urban Land Magazine where he penned two poems raising the concerns of minority contractors and the need for affordable housing. The survival of a harrowing near-death experience in the Mojave Desert in 2010 abruptly altered his focus away from economics toward the spiritual realm. The change is memorialized in his poetry manuscript "The Desert Hat" which is available at http://bit.ly/2fa3UYc

Ralph Thurston Seaton is a poet and artist who has published two books. He lived, studied and taught in NYC. His father was a magician from the islands.

Helen Seid has lived in Culver City since 1972 and well remembers all the places that she describes in her poem. She originally moved here so that her son and daughter could attend our wonderful schools. Helen worked at City Hall for the City Treasurer's Office for many years until she retired. Both Helen and her husband love to cruise and have traveled to over 100 countries, but, as Dorothy said "There's no place like home" although, as her poem tells us, it can change over the years.

Miriam Schnepp was born in Shanghai and attended British schools where students studied. As an English teacher at Culver schools she taught her classes to write poetry. She has written poetry for many years and is thought of as the poet in residence at the Senior Center

Lyra Brody Small, 9, is a 5th grader at Linwood Howe Elementary School. At school she was elected as a green seat, in which she educates her fellow Vikings about taking care of the earth. In addition to her regular subjects at school, she studies piano, violin, Spanish and French. When she was 4 she won the talent show with her hula hooping prowess at her Filipino family reunion in Iloilo, Philippines. In November 2016, she visited and reported on the Obama White House for KidScoop Media. Her article was published in multiple local and national newspapers. Lyra's passions are adventure, art and writing. She wrote *Missing Italy* after traveling to Capo d'Orlando, Sicily, as part of the Culver City Sister City Delegation in May 2017, with her family, including her dad Culver City Vice Mayor Thomas Small.

Sheila Steckler was a teacher of English as a Second Language in New York and taught while she was in the Peace Corps in Paraguay

Angie Waller—Originally from England, Angie has called Southern California home since 1975. She enjoys gardening, reading, movies, travel and is active in the Culver City Woman's Club

When **Marsha Wilde** was nine years old, her mother gave her a pad and pencil and suggested that rather than griping about the long wait to see an MD at a hospital clinic in New York City, Marsha write down her thoughts and feelings. She started to write and has never stopped.

Joanne Wolf is a 59 year Culver City resident. She was involved in Nursery School, the Culver City schools, Boy Scouts and was a Girl Scout Leader. She is a Marriage and Family Therapist (now retired) and has been a volunteer Therapist, now in her 11th year, at our Culver City High School's Sandy Segal Mental Health Center. She has been a member of the Culver City Senior Center since its opening and loves calling Culver City home.

Dr. Janet Cameron Hoult is Professor Emerita of Language Education at California State University, Los Angeles. In 1970, Dr. Hoult moved to Culver City which became her home base as she continued her travels all over the world. She attended high school in Iran, universities in Lebanon, France and the United States, and had teaching assignments in Germany, Korea, Japan, Thailand and China. She has published four books of poetry two of which have won awards BODY PARTS A Collection of Poems About Aging and Where Did the Sun Go? Myths and Legends of Solar Eclipses Around the World told with Poetry and Puppetry. In 2015 Janet was appointed Culver City's Honorary Artist Laureate for Poetry and conducted poetry readings and a contest for the 2017 Centennial.

The Culver City Historical Society

The Culver City Historical Society was created for the purpose of collecting, preserving and exhibiting the history, cultural and civic accomplishments of Culver City and its environs. These articles by Julie Lugo Cerra and Ryan Vincent, both active members, will provide readers of this poetry collection with background on our wonderful city and the Centennial Celebration.

Looking Back Winter 2017 — by Julie Lugo Cerra, City Historian

Culver City's Centennial year presents a wonderful opportunity for nostalgic looks back into our rich history. The last big celebration was the 75th Anniversary. Coordinated by the office of Syd Kronenthal, director of Parks and Recreation, the city formed a steering committee. It included Paul Jacobs, chair, Charles McCain, vice-chair, Susan Berg, secretary, and members Carolyn Cole, Jake Jakubowski, Syd Kronenthal, Carol Layana, Julie Lugo Cerra, Raechel Moskowitz, Steven J. Rose, Charles B. Smith and Albert Vera.

The group offered a broad scope of community expertise, which included city employees, elected officials (city and school board), commissioners, senior activists, Chamber of Commerce, YMCA, and Homeowners Association leaders. Several of the members' own history began in the Heart of Screenland. Local moviemaker Hal Roach, who was celebrating his 100th birthday that year, acted as the honorary chair.

That kickoff began on the steps of the Irving Thalberg Building on a historic movie lot (now Sony Pictures). Roger Mayer, then with Turner Entertainment, helped plan a Culver City Film Festival that featured selected short subjects and classic movies. The Chamber of Commerce sponsored a 75th Anniversary coffee table book. The Culver City News published a special oversize magazine with articles on the history of the city, and its many organizations, many of which took out ads to facilitate its publishing. The YMCA sold anniversary lapel pins, and that was just the tip of the iceberg! The 90th was also celebrated.

For the Centennial, a 501(c)3 was formed in 2016 to manage activities, official events and products. Jim Clarke (now mayor) was the first chair, followed by former mayor Paul Jacobs. A kickoff, parade, gala at Sony Pictures Studios, commemorative lapel pins sponsored by the YMCA, and creative logo items are symbolic of the spirit of the year. We look forward to visits from our city founder's family. Grandsons Chris Wilde, Dr. John Battle and family have been invited to represent the Culver family for the actual anniversary in September. Join the fun to celebrate our history. And think about items that should be included in a time capsule for our first hundred years!

Looking Back — Spring 2017 — by Julie Lugo Cerra

As a new year emerges full of promise, it also sends us back in time to think about accomplishments, our city's first hundred years, and its future. My interest in local history began with the Lugo Ranch, and was enhanced by a plea from my mother to "take your father to the new historical society." My dad, she suggested, "would be a natural." She was right, and it was fun!

The Society sparked my research on historic sites. The city had no ordinance to protect historic structures at that time, so in 1981 we were treading on uncharted waters. Politically, it was clear the city did not want to be restricted in issuing permits for structural or cosmetic changes. The bad news is that the 1928 City Hall is gone. The good news is that people can see the original plaque with names of the Board of Trustees at the time, from 1928 on the 3/4 façade entry to the current/same City Hall site, with updated information. In addition, the historic site plaque is read by many in the grassy area on the corner of Duquesne and Culver Boulevards.

Since then a Culver City Historic Preservation Advisory Committee (HPAC) was formed. Several society members served on the committee (including Judy Potik, Stephen Schwartz, Mary Ellen Fernandez, Carolyn Cole, and Jim Lamm). An Historic Preservation ordinance was passed by the City Council in 1990, and later, it was combined with Art in Public Places, codified and placed under a newly formed Cultural Affairs Commission. The results of that action can be seen on the city website and in plaques on historic structures like The Hull Building (CCHS Historic Site #2), The Citizen Building (CCHS Site #4), and many more. Artworks like the bronze lion sculpture fountain and the Culver Family in "A Moment In Time" (both of which can be found adjacent to The Culver Hotel) are examples of public art with a tie to local history.

Another benefit of local historic research is the cooperative City-Society partnership in providing tours. Our first bus tours were written for Fiesta La

Ballona. The city provided the bus and driver while the Society's contribution yielded the scripted route and trained docents. In the early days, we were often lucky to have Harry Culver's daughter, Patricia Culver Battle, join us on board the 55-minute runs. A big challenge became return route information after Washington Boulevard. Sites seemed sparse after we turned onto La Cienega Boulevard. My father, with a little gleam in his eye, suggested I translate the word "La Cienega" for the answer. Somehow my high school Spanish classes did not talk much about "swamps," but that became another bit of information to share!

As always, I encourage you to enjoy the benefits of our Culver City Historical Society. Visit the CCHS Archives, website, look for historic sites, the new bus wraps with historic photos, be active and share your insights into local history!

Culver City Finds Itself by Ryan Vincent

As we celebrate Culver City's Centennial, it's natural to wonder how the city came to be, and what it was like before 1917.

The quick history of pre-incorporated Culver City: Home to the Gabrielinos (nee Tongva) native peoples, and it was part of the ranchos that subdivided present-day Los Angeles County in the early 1800's. Barley, beans and grapes were the major cash crops, along with cattle and horses, but soon motion pictures became the city's industry. Harry Culver had already pinpointed the area that would make his real estate fortunes due to it being halfway between downtown Los Angeles and Abbot Kinney's "Venice of America" seaside resort, with the Pacific Electric Railway "Short Line" depot at Venice and Bagley Avenue already in place, and anounced his plans for a city at the California Club on July 22, 1913. Then Culver famously saw Thomas Ince filming a Western along Ballona Creek, convinced Ince to move his studio from Pacific Palisades to Washington Blvd. and Jasmine in 1915 where the colonnades of Ince/Triangle Studios still stand, and "The Heart of Screenland" was off and running.

To hear the *Los Angeles Evening Herald* tell it, the impetus for Harry Culver to seek a vote of incorporation for his new city wasn't to found a city bearing his name, to make his fortune, or to improve his standing in the region. Instead, it was the birth of his daughter.

A headline on August 13, 1917, in the *Herald* read, "Increase Culver City Population by 1; Ask Incorporation."

"That the population of Culver City had increased over night from 560 to 561 and that this was the main reason for the petition for incorporation of Culver City as a city of the sixth class, was the unique plea of Harry S. Culver to the board of county supervisors today. The increase in the population, Mr. Culver announced, was a new Culver, Miss Patricia by name and one day old."

On September 8, 1917, the *Herald* mentioned that the election was being held: "Polls opened at 6 this morning and will close this evening at 7. There are 560 residents in Culver City. Harry Culver, the founder of Culver City, predicted that the vote in favor of incorporation would be unanimous."

The next entry in the Herald about the nascent city was on September 12, 1917, with the headline, "Culver City Ready for Big Festival."

"The Culver City Chamber of Commerce is planning an all-day carnival to celebrate the city's incorporation and the sixteen-acre addition to the Triangle Film corporation's studio at that city, already the biggest studio in the world."

By 1918 Triangle Studios were sold to Samuel Goldwyn, with Ince already having moved to what is now The Culver Studios, with "The Mansion" (or "Colonial Administration Building") the first to be built on the lot, and in 1919 Hal Roach built his studio on Washington across from what is now the Culver City Expo Line station. In 1924 Goldwyn Pictures merged with Metro Pictures and Louis B. Mayer Pictures, forming Metro-Goldwyn-Mayer Studios, better known as MGM.

As for what Culver City was like prior to incorporation, the best we have is a photo with 1914 written on the photo itself by an anonymous cartographer. Culver Grammar School is now home to the Culver City Unified School District offices, next to Linwood E. Howe Elementary. Harry Culver's home was originally located on Delmas Terrace before it was moved to Cheviot Hills. The Culver Building and Hotel of course is the iconic triangular building at Culver and Main streets, which opened as the Hotel Hunt in 1924. "Club Hall" became the Legion Building, built in 1930, which still stands on Hughes Avenue, just south of Venice. Culver City Park is what's now Media Park, near Venice and Culver Boulevards. And the depot is what's now the Expo Line's Culver City Station.

Just as it's hard to imagine Culver City back when it was barley and bean fields, it's impossible to conceive of what the area will look like in another hundred years. We can only hope that it will still be going strong, and that its magnificent history will continue to be preserved and appreciated by people such as yourselves, our most valued members of the Culver City Historical Society.

The Culver City Historical Society

Michelle Bernardin, President 2010—2017
Hope Parrish 2017—

Mailing Address: P.O. Box 3428, Culver City, CA 90231-3428
ARC Address: 4117 Overland Ave., Culver City, CA 90230
Phones: (310) 253-6941 (310) 253-6942 Fax

Email: <u>info@culvercityhistoricalsociey.org</u> The Culver City Historical Society was created for the purpose of collecting, preserving and exhibiting the history, cultrural and civic accomlishments of Culver City and its environs. Located in the Veteran's Memorial Building at 4117 Overland Avenue, the Culver City Historical Society Archives and Resource Center (ARC) is open the 1st and 3rd Sundays of every month from 1:00 pm to 3:00 pm and by appointment. Please enter through the parking lot at the rear of the building.

Proceeds from the sale of this book will go to the Culver City Historical Society.

Acknowledgments

Culver City City Council
   Mayor — Jeffrey Cooper
   Vice-Mayor — Thomas Aujero Small
   Council Member — Jim B. Clarke
   Council Member — Goran Eriksson
   Council Member — Meghan Sahli-Wells

   City Manager — John Nachbar
   City Clerk — Jeremy Green
   City Attorney — Carol Schwab

Culver City Chamber of Commerce
   Resident/CEO — 2017 — Colin Diaz
   Resident/CEO — 1987-2017 — Steven Rose, In Memoriam

Culver City Centennial Celebration Committee
   Paul Jacobs, President — 2016-2017
   Jim B. Clarke, President — 2015-2016
   Darrel Menthe, Vice-President-Treasurer
   Judy Scott, Secretary
   Mike Cohen, Director
   Phil Tangalakis, Director
   Jozelle Smith, Director
   Marcus Tiggs, Director 2016-2017
   Andrew Weissman, Director
   Janice Beighey, Director
   Terry Robbins, Director 2015-2016
   Scott Wyant, Director 2015-2016, In Memoriam
   Kathleen Tepley, Advisor
   Julie Lugo Cerra, Advisor
   Shelly Wolfberg, City Liaison

LACG Centennial Celebration Team
   Kathleen Tepley, Founder/CEO Los Angeles Consulting Group
   Marie Kennedy (Website / Social Media / PR)
   Daniel Bickham
   Camille Taylor

The Culver City Historical Society
    Hope Parrish, President
    Julie Lugo Cerra, Culver City's Honorary Historian
    Matt Del-Hierro, Liaison

Culver City Cultural Affairs Commission
    Len Dickter, Chair
    Jeannine Wisnosky Stehlin, Vice Chair
    Tania Fleischer, Member
    Brenda G. Williams, Member
    Zoltan Pali, Member
    Serena Wright-Black, Administrative Services Director
    Christine Byers, Public Art and Historic Preservation Coordinator
    Susan Obrow, Special Events Coordinator

Centennial Poetry Readings:

Poetry and Pizza — October 8, 2016
    Culver City Senior Center
    Pizza provided by California Pizza Kitchen, Overland Ave., Culver City

Poetry and Pasta — April 8, 2017
    Culver City Julian Dixon Library
    Pasta provided by California Pizza Kitchen, Overland Ave., Culver City

Poetry, Popcorn and Pie — September 9, 2017
    Mayme Clayton Library and Museum (MCLM)
    Popcorn provided by MCLM
    Pie provided by Costco

Special Thanks for those assisting at the Venues
    Culver City Senior Center — Debbie Cahill, Program Director
    Culver City Julian Dixon Library — Laura Frakes, Librarian
        CC Friends of the Library
    Mayme Clayton Library and Museum — Lloyd Clayton, Director
        Steven Fisher, Non-Profit Director

Poets—Word Painting with Poetry Class at the Senior Center
        L.A. GOAL Poets
        Culver City Poets

Sandra Coopersmith—Consulting Editor

Poetry Book Sponsors —The Berman/Rutenberg Families

CPSIA information can be obtained
at www.ICGtesting.com
Printed in the USA
JSHW050021100623
42911JS00001B/153

9 781478 796152